# CONTENTS

# SYON

Syon House
Syon Park
Brentford
Middx TW8 8JF

**www.syonpark.co.uk**

# INTRODUCTION

by His Grace The Duke of Northumberland

# WELCOME TO SYON PARK

Syon House rose from monastic ashes after the English Reformation and became a Royal Palace during the latter Tudor era. In 1604, James I gave it to the 9th Earl of Northumberland for supporting James' claim to the English crown but in 1605 the Earl was implicated in the Gunpowder Plot to blow up the King and Parliament, and sent to the Tower of London. Fortunately, the Percy family managed to hang on to the house and, despite the attritions of war, taxation and the near extinction of the family name, it remains in our hands. Over the centuries, Syon was altered to suit the needs of different generations but the house and landscape have changed little since the late 18th century when the first Percy Duke and Duchess of Northumberland employed Robert Adam to design suitable interiors while Lancelot "Capability" Brown set to work redesigning the surrounding landscape.

Syon is still a family home and a verdant oasis within the bustling streets and roads of Greater London; the gardens and arboretum house rare and beautiful plants, the water meadows are home to a host of wildlife, the house contains a wonderful collection of art and furniture, and the Great Conservatory is an architectural gem, designed to house the 3rd Duke's extensive botanical collection. There is open space for recreation, 'Snakes and Ladders' for adventurous children, a garden centre for the green-fingered, a trout lake for the fly fisherman, the Syon Park Hotel with its spa, conference centre and fine restaurants, and many events that take place in the park and gardens.

My family and I welcome you to Syon and hope you enjoy this special place.

# THE SITE

*Syon Park is a remarkable survival of a privately owned rural estate, surrounded by a great city. It is situated between the two great arterial routes of the Thames and the main road west from London.*

Syon is a living landscape containing many elements of British history from prehistoric times to the present day. Many changes over the centuries have reflected the wealth and power of its owners, expressed through the latest trends and technologies in architecture and design. Syon is now the only part of the tidal Thames with water meadows and a natural foreshore, and it is likely that much of the site once formed an island, or eyot, in the Thames. In prehistory the stretch of the river around Syon was a mass of creeks, islands and marshes, and the line of the two lakes represents a prehistoric channel or palaeochannel.

There is evidence of Neolithic, Bronze Age and Iron Age activities in the area with the foreshore in front of Syon House producing a wealth of archaeological finds from metal objects to fish traps. It would have been possible to ford the Thames near Syon and it was here that Julius Caesar crossed in 54 BCE. The later Roman road from London to the West ran along the edge of the Park, and archaeological investigation has uncovered a substantial Roman settlement in this area. Later, there were Roman and Saxon settlements at Brentford, where the River Brent was forded by the main Roman road. In 1016 the Saxon King, Edmund Ironside, defeated the Danes at the Battle of Brentford.

To the south-west, Isleworth was recorded in the Domesday Book and during the 13th century Henry II's brother Richard, Earl of Cornwall, owned a manor house in the village. In 1415, King Henry V founded a Bridgettine Abbey at nearby Twickenham, dedicated to the 'Order of St Saviour, the Blessed Virgin Mary and St Bridget of Syon'. This site proved unsuitable and the abbey was moved to the site now occupied by Syon House. Construction commenced in 1426 and by 1431 the first buildings were ready for occupation. Syon Park is named after the abbey, which in turn took its name from Mount Zion in the Holy Land.

*These stakes were found on the foreshore near Brentford Dock during the early 1900s and were probably associated with an Iron Age or Roman settlement on the river. A claim was made at the time that they formed part of the British defences against Caesar.*

*A view of Brentford and the Thames foreshore during the Roman period. The site now occupied by Syon Park is on the bottom left of the picture.*

Painting by G. Manchester from '2000 years of Brentford' by Roy Canham, London 1978.

Syon House and its surroundings at the beginning
of the 18th century painted by Jan Griffier.

# SYON ABBEY
## (1415 - 1539)

*Syon Abbey was the only Bridgettine house in England in the 15th century. The Order had been founded in the 14th century by the Swedish mystic, St Bridget, or Birgitta, who established an abbey at Vadstena in Sweden. The Order was unusual in that it accommodated separate communities of men and women, each requiring entirely independent quarters for living and prayer. Intellectually and spiritually dynamic, the Bridgettines were a radical reformist movement within the Church, dedicated to private prayer and public preaching.*

The abbey consisted of 60 sisters in one community and 13 priests, 4 deacons and 8 lay brothers in the other. The Abbess ruled both communities in all temporal affairs and the Confessor-General was responsible for spiritual direction. Recent archaeological investigations by Time Team and the University of London have revealed the great abbey church to lie between Syon House and the river, with the cloisters and associated buildings on either side. The eastern wall of the church stood between modern Syon House and the river, but the western end of the church has not been located and so the actual size of the building remains a matter of conjecture.

Modern research has revealed a great deal about the priests and nuns of Syon. Many of the sisters were of aristocratic birth, and would have included some of the most educated women in the country. The priests were often semi-retired academics – particularly from Cambridge – and they gathered a formidable library, which was to become one of the finest in England. The abbey was a large complex, with accommodation for the many noble patrons who spent time here, and stood in 30 acres of orchard and gardens.

*The Lady Abbess of Syon Abbey, South Brent, Devon with the iron cross and the pinnacle from the original abbey gateway at Syon.*

Syon Abbey was at the time of its suppression in 1539 the tenth wealthiest in England. It was endowed with estates as far afield as St Michael's Mount in Cornwall and the 'messuage, land, meadow, wood, pasture and rent in Istelworth, Twykenham, Worton and Heston, with their appurtenances aforesaid, in free and perpetual alms for ever'. The priests of Syon Abbey were renowned for their rigorous intellectualism and learning, and the abbey became a major site of pilgrimage and public preaching.

There were large courtyards under the west lawn of Syon House, where the brethren of Syon would have preached – in English – to the assembled pilgrims. Such a wealthy and influential institution inevitably became embroiled in the religious turmoil of the reign of King Henry VIII. Syon was situated across the river from the great Tudor Palace at Richmond and Queen Catherine of Aragon was a regular visitor, as were Anne Boleyn and Jane Seymour. In 1534 the abbey became connected with Elizabeth Barton 'the Holy Maid of Kent'. She had particularly angered King Henry VIII with visions denouncing his divorce from Queen Catherine, and meetings were arranged at Syon between Barton and Sir Thomas More.

There was great resistance to Henry's plans at Syon, both among the priests and the nuns, and Government agents intent on suppressing the abbey made an exaggerated report 'certefying the Incontynensye of the Nunnes of Syon with the Friores'. Richard Reynolds, one of the priests, refused to acknowledge the King's supremacy and in 1535 he was charged as a traitor along with three

*Syon Abbey as it is believed to have looked by Dr Jonathan Foyle.*

*The Visitation and surrender of Syon Nunnery to the Commissioners, 1539 by Paul Falconer Poole (1807-79). Courtesy of City of Bristol Museum & Art Gallery/Bridgeman Art Library*

Carthusian priests and John Hale, the vicar of Isleworth. The penalty for this was hanging, drawing and quartering, which was carried out on each man in turn. Reynolds was the last to die as his fellows were butchered and "seeing them cruelly quartered and their bowels taken out, preached unto them and comforted them promising a heavenly banquet and supper for their sharp breakfast taken for their Master's sake". Reynold's head is said to have been placed on the abbey gateway, and he was later canonised as a martyr.

At the time of its suppression in 1539, the abbey had a community of 73 members, and many of them remained together in exile, whether in England or abroad. In 1557 the nuns were recalled by Queen Mary I to re-establish themselves at Syon, but this restoration was short lived and, they left the country once more on the accession of Queen Elizabeth I, finally settling in Portugal in 1594. There they stayed until 1861 when they returned to England and settled in Devon, where they lived and prayed as the only English community of religious women in continuous existence since before the reformation. It is said that Abbess Jordan never surrendered the keys or common seal of Syon at the Suppression. When the 2nd Duke of Northumberland visited the Order in Lisbon, the Lady Abbess of the time remarked that she still had the keys of Syon, to which the Duke replied '*Indeed Madam? But I have altered the locks since then*'.

*Celebration of the 600th anniversary of the foundation of Syon Abbey in 2015. The Bridgettine community of Syon were dissolved as recently as 2011.*

# DAILY LIFE AT SYON ABBEY

*The most important element of daily life was the Divine Office, celebrated seven times a day. Although the two communities at Syon were strictly segregated, they came together at these times to praise God, the Brothers behind the High Altar and the Sisters above the Nave. The day started at about 5am, when the Brothers assembled in the church to sing Matins and Lauds, the Sisters following on in their choir. Masses would be celebrated and further Offices sung, after which at about 9.30am there was time for a 'collation', probably bread and water; a more substantial breakfast was provided for the sick, the elderly, the young and for those engaged in heavy work. Following the next Office (Sext), High Mass was held and after mid-day prayers the two communities would proceed to their respective refectories for dinner, the main meal of the day. It was the duty of the Cellaress to provide food and drink for everyone 'sick and whole', and each day she was to order meat, fish and vegetables 'as far as the market and purse will stretch'. During the afternoon, there was time for study, needlework or manual work, and the sisters were allowed to speak until Evensong. Silence was strictly kept in the church choir, refectory, cloister and dormitory and always in the washing house. Signs were used wherever possible but it was permissible to speak in a whisper if really necessary.*

**Candle** – *make the signe of buttur and the signe for daye*
**Dissh** – *make a cercle with thy right forfynger in the myddes of thy left palme*
**Milke** – *drawe thy left little fynger in maner of mylkyng*
**Syngyng** – *bowe the fyngyrs of thy right hande and move them to and fro afore thy mouthe*
**Wyne** – *move thy forefinger up and downe upon the ende of thy thumbe afore thy eye*

*At about 5pm, the Brothers would gather in the church for Evensong, the Sisters again following on. Shortly after supper, bells would call the Sisters to 'spiritual collation' in the Chapter House, where announcements would be made and a reading given from a holy book. During this time, the Brothers sang Compline. When their reading was over, the Sisters, too, sang Compline in their Choir. This was the last communal prayer of the day: a Blessing with Holy Water was given, and everyone then retired to the dormitories at around 8.30pm. Silence was strictly observed until after Lady Mass the following morning.*

*Background image: Abbess Jordan from Aungier's 'History of Syon Monastery, Isleworth & Hounslow'.*

# THE TUDORS & SYON

*After the suppression of the abbey in 1539, the estate became Crown property. Catherine Howard, fifth wife of King Henry VIII was confined at Syon where she was allocated two rooms 'furnished moderately as her life and condition hath deserved', before her execution in 1542. In 1547, the Duke of Somerset, the Lord Protector to the young King Edward VI, took possession of the estate.*

While some landmarks from the abbey were still standing at this time, much of the complex had already been demolished, and many materials would have been recycled into the structure of Somerset's grand new house, a brick building faced with white stone. Somerset essentially built the house we see today, a grand mansion around a central courtyard, but probably retaining elements of the abbey complex as service buildings. Formal gardens in the latest Italian style stretched towards the river, with terraces and walks, and the view of the house from the river, as the great and good of the country travelled by water between London and the great Tudor palace at Richmond, would have been of central importance.

However, Tudor politics was full of dangers and Somerset was accused of plotting against the Crown and executed in 1552. Syon was then acquired by one of his rivals, John Dudley, Duke of

*Portrait of a lady thought to be Lady Jane Grey.*

Northumberland. The Duke's son, Lord Guildford Dudley, had married Lady Jane Grey, great-granddaughter of King Henry VII, and it was at Syon in 1553 that she was formally offered the Crown by the Duke, as a protestant candidate for the throne. She accepted reluctantly, was conveyed to London by river and proclaimed Queen. Nine days later she was displaced by the catholic Mary Tudor, and the following year she was executed.

Syon reverted to the Crown in 1558 and an inventory of 1593 describes a substantial Tudor house large enough to accommodate the Queen and her Court.

*The Lord Protector Somerset.*

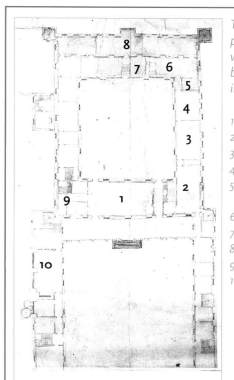

*The earliest known plan of the house with room layout based on a 1593 inventory.*

1. Hall
2. Great Chamber
3. Presence Chamber
4. Privy Chamber
5. Withdrawing Chamber
6. Bedchamber
7. Coffer Chamber
8. Long Gallery
9. Buttery & Pantry
10. Kitchens

When King Henry VIII died in 1547 his coffin lay for the night at Syon on its way from Westminster to Windsor. A curious prophecy was then fulfilled. In 1535, a Franciscan friar, named William Peto, when preaching before King Henry VIII, had declared 'that God's judgements were ready to fall upon his head ... and that the dogs would lick his blood as they had done Ahab's' ... Peto's prediction came true when the coffin rested at Syon as a dog was found licking up certain remains which had managed to seep through the coffin from the bloated corpse inside. This was regarded by some as a divine judgement upon the King for his desecration of the abbey.

*"[T]he pavement of the church was wetted with Henry's blood. In the morning came plumbers to solder the coffin under whose feet was suddenly seen a dog creeping and licking up the king's blood. If you ask me how I know this, I answer William Grenville, who could scarcely drive away the dog told me and so did the plumber also."*

*Tudor Funeral Procession.*

11

Henry, 9th Earl

Josceline, 11th Earl

Elizabeth Percy

Algernon, 10th Earl

Thomas, 7th Earl

SIR HENRY PERCY (HOTSPUR.) 1402.

Elizabeth, 11th Countess

Hugh Percy as a boy

Algernon Percy, 4th Duke

# THE PERCY FAMILY

## THE EARLS AND THE DUKES OF NORTHUMBERLAND

Hugh & Charlotte 3rd Duke & Duchess

George, 5th Duke

Hugh Smithson & Elizabeth Seymour, 1st Duke & Duchess

Hugh & Frances 2nd Duke & Duchess

Algernon Seymour, 7th Duke of Somerset

Algernon Percy, 6th Duke

Alan Ian & Helen, 8th Duke & Duchess

Hugh & Elizabeth, 10th Duke & Duchess

Ralph & Jane, The present Duke & Duchess

Henry George, 7th Duke

George, 9th Duke

Henry Percy, 11th Duke

# THE PERCY FAMILY

*Henry, 9th Earl of Northumberland (1564-1632), the first Percy to possess Syon, took great pride in his family history, tracing his ancestry back to the Emperor Charlemagne. William de Percy (d.1096) came to England around the time of the Norman Conquest and over the following centuries the Percys established great estates north and south, principally in Sussex, Yorkshire, Lincolnshire, Cumberland and Northumberland. By the late 14th century, in the time of Sir Henry Percy, nicknamed Harry Hotspur, the Percys were at the height of their powers, making and breaking kings. Through the civil conflicts of the 15th century and the political and religious twists of the 16th century, the line experienced deaths on the battlefield, executions at the block, dispossessions through attainder and murder in the Tower of London.*

The 9th Earl's extraordinary life followed the course of a true Renaissance nobleman, despite his deafness and 15 years as a prisoner. The Earl had a love of learning and books, and developed a fine library with the assistance of scholars such as Thomas Harriot. Like many lively and enquiring minds of his time, he was drawn to alchemy, hence his nickname of the 'Wizard Earl'. There was a strong element of the Elizabethan adventurer in him and he took his band of military retainers on at least two expeditions to wars in the Low Countries. He was interested in the New World and with friends such as Sir Walter Raleigh consumed great quantities of tobacco and enjoyed potatoes on his household menu.

November 4th 1605, Thomas dined with the Earl at Syon and the next day the plot to blow up the Houses of Parliament was discovered. Thomas Percy was one of the principal plotters and was shot dead trying to make his escape from Holbeach House in Warwickshire. The Earl was immediately implicated through his association with Thomas and the fateful meeting at Syon. Though pleading his innocence, he was arrested, fined a massive £30,000, and imprisoned in the Tower of London for 15 years. There he occupied the Martin Tower in some style - the accounts reveal that he kept twenty servants, a barber and a cutter

In 1594 the Earl acquired Syon through his marriage to Dorothy Devereux when Queen Elizabeth granted him a leasehold of the property. His support for James I on the death of Queen Elizabeth in 1603 brought even greater influence and wealth, and he was gifted the freehold of the Syon estate in 1604. However, from this high point the Earl's fortunes were to change dramatically. A distant cousin, Thomas Percy, was the constable of the Earl's castle at Alnwick and had responsibility for administering the castle and its estates, as well as acting as his messenger to the Scottish court. Thomas was a staunch Catholic and one of the 'Gentlemen Pensioners' of whom the Earl was captain. On

*HENRY, 9TH EARL*
*(1584-1632)*

gardens within the Tower, duly tended by a gardener from Syon. He built a bowling alley and became an expert at shove-halfpenny! The Earl was renowned in the Tower for his experiments in distilling alcohol, and, with deliveries of fruit from Syon, captivity was perhaps not excessively arduous and he was also able to re-acquaint himself with his old friend Sir Walter Raleigh, a fellow prisoner. In 1617, the native American princess, Pocahontas, lived in Brentford and was a guest at Syon House.

*The early 17th century archway named after the 9th Earl which today stands within the area occupied by the Garden Centre.*

for his corns! New clothes were purchased and copious quantities of wine and tobacco were consumed during his imprisonment. More than £200 was spent on wine and almost £50 on tobacco in one year, the modern equivalent of more than £25,000 on wine and £6,000 on tobacco. The Earl created a laboratory and library, with books brought from Syon, and skeletons supplied by his physician, as well as 'retorts, crucibles, alembics, zodiacal charts and globes'. For recreation he made a pathway, thereafter known as 'Northumberland's Walk' and busied himself with laying out

*Ætatis suæ 21. A°.1616.*

*Portrait of Pocohontas. After Simon van de Passe (1595 - 1647). By kind permission of National Portrait Gallery, Smithsonian Institution.*

*Two contemporary engravings depicting Thomas Percy's involvement with the Gunpowder Plot of 1605. Below, Thomas is seen fifth from left, with Guido (Guy) Fawkes to the right. Below right, an engraving with vignettes describing his capture and death.*

The Earl carried out significant improvements to both the house and grounds at Syon, even during his imprisonment, with around £9,000 spent on the Estate and a further £5,000 on the house, including a bath house for the Countess. A Mr Styckles was introduced "to give direction for garden work" and a new walled garden was laid out with rose-trees and a variety of fruit trees, notably cherry, apricot, mulberry and quince. Other additions included a grape house, and a "nightingale garden", probably all between Syon House and the Thames. On his release from the Tower in 1621, the Earl was confined to his estate at Petworth, where he died on November 5th 1632.

Thomas Harriot was the greatest English mathematician and astronomer of his time. He had been a long-time acquaintance of Sir Walter Raleigh, through whose influence he had become a pensioner of the 9th Earl. When the Earl was imprisoned, he gave Harriot use of the laboratory and a sleeping apartment in the Martin Tower. Harriot then moved to a house at Syon, and it was here at 9 am on July 26th 1609, that he became the first person to map the moon, using a simple telescope. He also went on to make notable observations such as sunspots, the satellites surrounding Jupiter, and the planet Mercury.

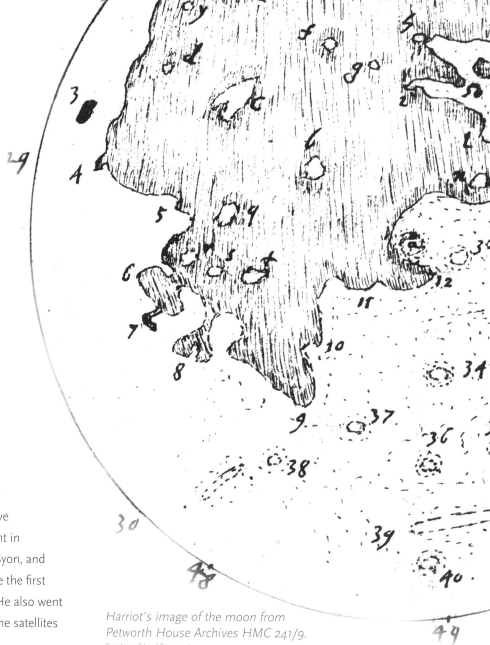

*Harriot's image of the moon from Petworth House Archives HMC 241/9.*
Courtesy of Lord Egremont.

*Battle of Brentford by John Hassall. One of a pair commissioned by Col. Grant Morden MP.*
*By kind premission of Hounslow Library Service Local Collections.*

# ALGERNON, 10TH EARL (1632 - 1668)

*The 10th Earl's life was founded on a most unusual education, with his father building a schoolroom at the Tower, where he was instructed by the poet, William Warner. Books for study were brought from Syon, and the young Algernon lodged in Tower Hill where he kept a pet fox.*

Algernon inherited from his father a great love of learning and of fine art, supporting the foremost artists of the day, principally Anthony Van Dyck and Peter Lely, and assembling an impressive collection of old masters. The fruits of his commissions and acquisitions can be seen today in the collections at Syon, Alnwick and Petworth. Lord High Admiral and President of the Council of War under King Charles I, Algernon held back from full commitment to the Royalist cause in the early days of the Civil War and so lost his commands. Yet the war came close to home at the Battle of Brentford on 12th November 1642, as Parliamentarian forces attempted to stop the king's march on London. The Royalist general, Prince Rupert, made Syon House his headquarters during the battle, and there was a heated exchange of fire with several ships and barges on the river and repairs subsequently had to be made to the house 'where it was shot through with ordnance'. The Parliamentarian forces were outnumbered and retreated to the river where some were drowned and others, including the radical John Lilburne, were forced to surrender. The victorious Royalist troops ransacked the houses and taverns of Brentford but their march on London was halted the following day by a parliamentarian army at Turnham Green.

*Syon House in the early 17th century. Built of Dunstable stone it was referred to as the 'white house'.*

Algernon supported a compromise between King and people which established his reputation for impartiality. After the King was arrested and imprisoned, the Earl was made governor to James, Duke of York and the younger royal children from 1646-1649. King Charles I, when held at Hampton Court, was able to visit the children at Syon.

*'Syon House, August 23, 1647: His Majesty came hither to see his children this morning early, with one troop of Horse, and the Commissioners, and dined here. August 29, 1647 The King hunted in Richmond Park, and afterwards dined here with his children at Syon'.*

King Charles I and the Duke of York, by Peter Lely, which now hangs in the Red Drawing Room, is thought to have been painted during one of the king's visits to Syon.

*The younger children of Charles I, after the Van Dyck at Windsor Castle.*

*King Charles I and The Duke of York.*

The house was used for a Council meeting by Cromwell in 1647 and also in 1665 by King Charles II, when the Plague was raging in London. The writer John Evelyn commented "when business was over I viewed that seat of the Earl of Northumberland, built out of an old Nunnery of stone and fair enough, but more celebrated for its garden than it deserves, yet there is excellent wall fruite and a pretty fountain, nothing else extraordinary". The 10th Earl retired to Syon and carried on developing the gardens, introducing many new and rare plants, as well as continuing to improve the orchards and kitchen gardens. There are records of artichokes, asparagus, melons and strawberries, as well as grapes, cherries, and more humble produce.

# THE SEYMOURS

*The Percys emerged in the Restoration period with their vast estates intact, until the death of the young 11th Earl, Josceline (1668-1670) who left an infant daughter, Elizabeth, as his sole heir. Elizabeth Percy had to face many ordeals, including a dispute over her guardianship in which her grandmother, Elizabeth Howard, widow of the 10th Earl, triumphed over her mother, Elizabeth Wriothesley, widow of Josceline.*

Since Elizabeth was a most eligible young heiress, her grandmother was busy from the time the girl reached the age of 12 brokering a suitable match and three marriages were contracted between 1679 and 1682. The first to Henry, Earl of Ogle, who died within six months, then to Thomas Thynne, from whom Elizabeth fled abroad and who was later murdered, and finally to the young Charles Seymour, the 6th Duke of Somerset, who became known as the 'Proud Duke'. It was at this time that Syon House was used by William III and Queen Mary II while marching on London during the Glorious Revolution of 1688. Elizabeth was a close friend of Princess Anne, later to become queen, and when Anne quarrelled with her sister Queen Mary, who objected to her friendship with the Duchess of Marlborough, the Duke and Duchess placed Syon at her disposal. While in residence at Syon in 1692 the princess gave birth to a son, George, but he died within hours.

*Petworth House, West Sussex.*
*By Kind permission of David Sellman.*

*Elizabeth Percy.*

Charles Seymour and Elizabeth Percy were prominent courtiers and held a series of influential posts. When Anne became Queen, the Duchess was appointed her Mistress of the Stole and Charles Seymour was Master of the Horse. His interests were widespread: he restored Petworth House in Sussex using his wife's money, bought paintings and silverware, patronised artists, especially Michael Dahl, and enjoyed racing at Newmarket. The Duke and Duchess would often stay at Syon when travelling from Petworth to London but it was primarily a summer residence and would be prepared for their arrival, with servants arriving by barge to install gilt leather and damask hangings, paintings, curtains and beds.

*The 6th Duke and Duchess of Somerset.*

In 1715, the Duke's son and heir Algernon, adjutant to the Duke of Marlborough, married Frances Thynne of Longleat, a 'blue stocking' of her age and a patron of poets and hymnwriters. She was profoundly disliked by her father-in-law, and the death in 1744 of their only son George, Lord Beauchamp, while on Grand Tour in Italy, provoked a family crisis as the 6th Duke moved to disinherit Algernon's surviving child, Elizabeth, so as to favour his other grandsons, the children of Sir William Wyndham. Algernon, however, fought back against the disinheritance of his daughter, taking his cause personally to King George II who judged that the great Northumberland estates must remain with Algernon's issue along with Northumberland House and Syon. Wyndham, however, succeeded on Algernon's death to vast lands in Sussex, Yorkshire and Cumberland.

The lives of Elizabeth Seymour and her husband Sir Hugh Smithson had been transformed by the death of her brother in 1744. Unusually for the age, theirs was a love match, and after their marriage in 1740 they lived at Stanwick, near Richmond, Yorkshire where he managed his estates and attended Parliament, while she concerned herself with running a provincial household.

*The reign of Algernon the 7th Duke of Somerset (1748-1750), though short, was significant. A warm-hearted family man (pictured above with his wife and daughter), he had always preferred his Percy ancestry and it was he who raised the statant lion, a Percy symbol, above the entrance to Northumberland House. After the demolition of Northumberland House in 1874, the lion was brought to Syon to grace the top of the eastern façade. In his moves towards improvement, this Duke had an admirable ally in his son-in-law Sir Hugh Smithson who, with his wife Elizabeth, used Syon as his southern residence.*

# THE 1st DUKE AND DUCHESS OF NORTHUMBERLAND

*Sir Hugh Smithson inherited the Percy estates and the title of Earl of Northumberland in 1750 and reigned as Earl and Duke (created 1766) of Northumberland until 1786. His marriage, title and vast inheritance thrust him to the forefront of the nobility and the nation's affairs. Elizabeth, 1st Duchess, was very proud of her Percy ancestry and totally committed to her husband's schemes, keeping an eye on the restoration work at Syon, which she reported to her husband in her letters. She liked to travel from London to Syon by state barge, being serenaded on the way by musicians. A great collector and commentator, she left a fascinating record of her life and times in her diaries.*

The Duke brought experience, mature judgement and an acute and enquiring mind to his task of modernising the Percy lands and properties. As a courtier his great interest in science was acknowledged and if the chimneys of Kensington Palace smoked, it was his advice that was sought. He transformed and modernised the administration of his estates, enclosed and planted woodlands, and exploited the industrial potential of his lands, particularly coal mining. He invested income from improved rents in the restoration of the principal Percy seats: Northumberland House, Alnwick Castle and Syon House.

*"Lady Tyrconnel had a dreadful fever. Her nurse imagining her to be asleep left her, a Washerwoman & a man passing along ye street a flower pot fell at their Feet on looking up they saw her 2 Legs out of the window She having only her Shift on. They had the presence of mind not to scream out But the man ask'd her the matter she said she was unjustly accused of Adultery & flying fm an enraged husband he promised to assist her & thus kept her in Talk till the woman knock'd at the Door & alarm'd the Servants who secured her."*

From the diary of the 1st Duchess of Northumberland Wednesday 28th July 1762.

The Duke and Duchess were determined to make their mark on Syon, as the house was somewhat old-fashioned and dilapidated and the grounds had never recovered from an excessively hard frost in 1739, which killed many trees, robbing the formal grounds of much of their structure. The solution was a complete redesign of the estate, with the Scottish architect, Robert Adam instructed to remodel the interior of the house and the Northumbrian designer, Lancelot "Capability" Brown, called upon to complete the transformation of the grounds in the fashionable style of the English Landscape Movement. Brown and Adam had more in common than just being the fashionable designers of their day, both were aspiring to create a new, ideal form of an earlier time.

Thus while Adam's architecture was inspired by Classical Rome, so Brown took the mediaeval deer park as a model for an ideal countryside, both consciously borrowing the connotations of wealth, power and antiquity, and packaging them for their clients. The Duke was one of Robert Adam's chief patrons and engaged him on his return from Italy in 1758. In 1761, Adam published his plan for the interior decoration of Syon House. This included a design for a complete suite of rooms on the principal level, together with a rotunda to be erected in the main courtyard. In the event, five main rooms on the west, south and east sides of the house, stretching from the hall to the gallery, were refurbished in a classical style. Adam's plans were put into effect by a team of craftsmen and artists, and antique statuary was imported from Rome by his brother, James, as were the scagliola columns in the Ante Room and the three great bronze statues by Luigi Valadier in the Hall and Ante Room.

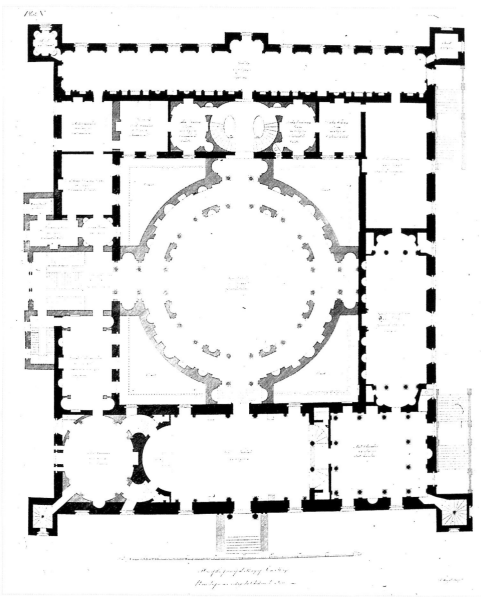

Robert Adam's plan for Syon which was never completed. The rotunda in the Courtyard was intended for entertaining.

Receipt for seeds and gardening tools 1764.

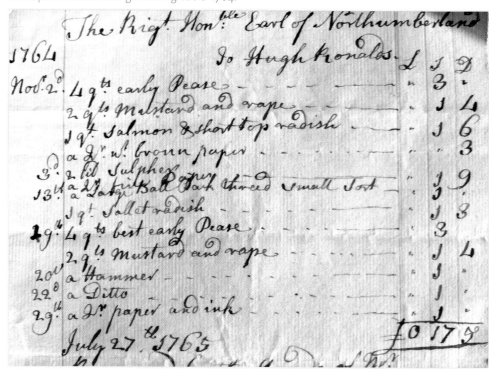

*The children of the 2nd Duke of Northumberland in the gardens at Syon.*

Hugh, the 2nd Duke (1786-1817), made the army his career. As a lad of 16, he raised a company of recruits from Alnwick to serve in the army with him in the Seven Years War, where they fought in the battles of Bergen and Minden in 1759. He later served with distinction as a general in the War of American Independence, where he was popular with ordinary soldiers on account of his concern for their welfare. At Syon, the 2nd Duke consolidated the restoration work of his father, instructing James Wyatt to build a new stable block and coach house and also the iron bridge over the outer lake at the west end of the Lime Avenue. The Duke also continued the development of the plant collection. American plants were fashionable at this time, and many were planted in the Wilderness Garden, which was now extended as far as Isleworth, where a menagerie had been built in 1760. Golden pheasants were sent from Longleat in 1773 to join swans, geese, guinea fowl and ducks, and even a bear, with its own attendant servant. In 1803 the architect Robert Mylne began work on an ornamental pavilion with an adjoining boat house for the state barge. Head gardeners included James Meader, who wrote The Planter's Guide in 1779 before going on to Russia where he served Catherine the Great in her 'English' Garden at Tsarskoe Selo, and William Forsyth who became a royal gardener. During most of his reign, the 2nd Duke was served by Thomas Hoy, who is buried in the graveyard of Isleworth Parish Church. The plants Forsythia and Hoya were named in honour of these last two gardeners.

*The Iron Bridge over the Outer Lake was designed by James Wyatt in 1790, and restored in 2012.*

The inheritance which the 2nd Duke left to his eldest son Hugh, 3rd Duke (1817-1847), made him the richest commoner in Britain, with huge royalties from wayleaves and from the docks and coal mines of the north-east, as well as an immense estate rental.

A courtier, who inherited his father's loyalty to the Prince Regent, the Duke was rewarded by King George IV with the honour of being the King's personal representative at the coronation of King Charles X of France in 1825. It was an occasion which called for a display of dazzle and glitter which the Duke could comfortably undertake from his own immense wealth. Later, in 1829-1830, the same lavishness and display of patronage accompanied the Duke's Vice Regency of Ireland.

*Hugh, 3rd Duke of Northumberland by Richard Dighton.*

*The Great Conservatory at Syon*

The power and influence of the Percys was confirmed when Duchess Charlotte Florentia was appointed as official governess to the young Princess Victoria. This role, which the Duchess fulfilled for six years until the coronation, included overseeing the Princess' education and accompanying her on court occasions. On Victoria becoming Queen in 1837, the Duke of Wellington wrote to the Duchess *'I have returned from the council at Kensington so delighted with your pupil that I can not deny myself the gratification of letting you know what an impression Her Majesty made on the Council at large.'*

The Duchess called Syon *'this delicious place'*, ranking it above all other residences and they carried out an extensive programme of works. The house was restored and provided with every amenity.

The architect, Thomas Cundy, provided the chief entrance to the house with a porte-cochère, the north wing was rebuilt, and the whole building clad in Bath stone. The lead hoppers and downpipes on the outside of Syon House are individually dated, and it is possible from these to track the progress of the works.

This Duke was fascinated by gardening, and in the 1820s the technologically innovative conservatory was built, and the gardens brought to a state of near horticultural perfection. He was a patron of influential writers such as John Claudius Loudon, who dedicated his Arboretum et Fruticetum Britannicum to him. This work includes numerous illustrations of trees growing at Syon, and Loudon acknowledged the encouragement the Duke had always given to gardening and *'more especially to the introduction and cultivation of foreign trees and shrubs.'*

*Queen Victoria in 1838, painted one year after she ascended the throne by the American Thomas Sully.*

When Algernon, 4th Duke (1847-1865) succeeded his brother, he was already a man of mature judgement and became known as 'Algernon the Good'. He served as a naval officer in the Napoleonic Wars and later as First Lord of the Admiralty in Lord Derby's administration (1852). Politically enlightened, his aim as a great landowner was to provide well for his tenants and to make his possessions an amenity for the wider community to enjoy. He opened up his parks and gardens, sent his artisans and labourers to London to see the Great Exhibition of 1851, and in the summer of that year opened Syon House and Northumberland House to the public. When the giant waterlily Victoria amazonica was propagated at Syon for the first time in Britain, it was exhibited at the Great Exhibition and taken on a tour of different cities.

During his reign, Giovanni Montiroli, the Italian architect who oversaw work at Alnwick Castle, was commissioned to design the ceilings in the Print Room, Green Drawing Room and Private Dining Room. Throughout the 19th century Syon continued to be maintained as a rural aristocratic estate. Horticultural triumphs included the first ripe mangosteens and coconuts to be produced

Victoria amazonica growing at Syon.
Reproduced by kind permission of The Linnaean Society.

in the country, as well as cloves, nutmeg, cocoa and vanilla. Fruit was sent to Alnwick and a Syon gardener regularly travelled to London to tend the window boxes of the family's town house.

By the end of the century, an article in Country Life recorded *'On every hand something will arrest attention. The trees are magnificent, ash, beech, elm and chestnut spreading their noble arms to cast shadows over the grass. Spacious lawns surround the house, and in the background on either side are bold sweeping shrubberies.....It is impossible to mention every valuable tree at Syon'.*

*Wyatt Bridge.*

*Helen, 8th Duchess of Northumberland by Philip de Laszlo.*

George, 5th Duke (1865-1867), first cousin of the 3rd and 4th Dukes, succeeded in 1865 at the great age of 87, and was followed on his death two years later by his son, Algernon, 6th Duke (1867-1899), who married Louisa, daughter and heiress of Henry Drummond, banker, political philosopher and religious reformer. The Duke and Duchess followed Drummond as prominent members of the Catholic Apostolic movement and inherited his Surrey estate at Albury Park, with its famous Evelyn gardens and church of the Catholic Apostolic sect.

Both the 6th Duke and his son Henry George, 7th Duke (1899-1918) were courtiers and active politicians. During the First World War the Riding School was converted into hospital ward accommodation and the house was placed at the disposal of the British Red Cross Society.

The 8th Duke, Alan Ian (1918-1930), was a career soldier, who fought in the Boer War and First World War. The social and political disruption resulting from the war left its mark on Syon: the growth of London led to development along the Great West Road, and the park itself came under threat from a proposed sewage works. Large private estates were proving increasingly costly to run, but the fact that the family still used Syon as one of their principal residences meant that the estate survived the economic crises of the 1930s and continued to provide much-needed local employment. The burden of providing leadership to the family during the 8th Duke's illness and the 9th Duke's minority thereafter fell to the remarkable Helen, Duchess, a daughter of the Duke of Richmond. She was an active promoter of the family's interest at both local and national level for more than half a century, from her marriage in 1911 to her death in 1965. She served Queen Elizabeth the Queen Mother for many years as Mistress of the Robes.

*A number of the books in the Long Gallery were from Henry Drummond's collection and came into Syon's possession through the marriage of his daughter, Louisa and Algernon, 6th Duke.*

During the Second World War George, the 9th Duke, (1930-1940), offered a wing of Syon House as accommodation for Guards officers, one of whom recalled: 'George Northumberland kindly opened a wing of his house at Sion. There we were to live in the greatest elegance – but in great discomfort from the intense cold.' The Duke was killed in action in Northern France at the age of 29, fighting a rearguard action with the Grenadier Guards during the retreat to Dunkirk.

During the war incendiary bombs caused damage to the park and house and when the nearby West Middlesex Hospital was hit, Syon House was offered to the nurses as accommodation. Syon House itself was hit by bombs, with extensive damage to the Ante Room, and a "doodlebug" V-1 flying bomb destroyed Ferry House at the Isleworth end of the Park.

In July 1944 VI flying bombs landed in Syon Park. On 3 Jul damage was caused to Syon House and 90 other houses by a bomb. On 4 Jul another bomb exploded in the Tide Meadow, about 600 yards from the ferry. 7 Jul, a further flying bomb exploded some 30 yards from the boundary wall within Park Road damaging 250 houses. (SCP, p26)

A summary of bombs at Syon from 1940 to 1945 is given in Ducal Papers:
    65 H.E. in Grounds
    1 Oil Bomb on wall at Dairy
    1 Shell damaged top of Conservatory

14 Bombs dropped in one night from Canal Bridge to Angel, Brentford. Two of these, one 1,000 lbs and one 500 lbs were in Garden at top of lane. The 1,000 lb. one was alive.

3 Flying bombs in one week. Rocket blast broke several windows. (38 killed, 280 injured at Pyrene).

270 Windows were broken when War ended.

9 Windows escaped damage.

4 Lots of incendiary bombs. On one occasion 1,500 cases were picked up in garden but only one on roof and one on muniment rooms. Several trees caught alight.

15 Flying bombs fell in Isleworth Parish.

## 24-years-old daughter of the Duke and Duchess of Buccleuch and Queensberry, will marry Lord Hugh Percy, Duke of Northumberland.

The 31-years-old Duke of Northumberland, who is Lord-in-Waiting to the King, is said to have ridden his black hunter for four days more than 100 miles to propose to Lady Elizabeth in her castle in Dumfriesshire

The reign of the 10th Duke, Hugh (1940-1988) saw the successful transformation of a great estate to meet the changing requirements of the second half of the 20th century. The Duke was a keen agriculturist, and served as chair of the Medical Research Council and Steward of the Royal Household. In 1946, the Duke married Elizabeth Montagu Douglas Scott, daughter of the Duke of Buccleuch; they had six children. Duke Hugh had a deep affection for Syon. After the war, he used Syon as his regular summer seat and opened the house for public viewing in 1951. The Great Conservatory became the focus of the gradual regeneration of the gardens and the Duke sought to finance this work through a National Garden Exhibition in partnership with ICI, culminating in 1968 with the opening of the Gardening Centre Ltd. This included the conversion of the former Riding School and stable complex into a garden centre, and the introduction of display gardens within the pleasure grounds.

Henry, the 11th Duke (1988-1995) worked in the film industry and made Syon his permanent home. In 1994 he opened the outer lake in the park as a trout fishery. His brother and successor Ralph, the present 12th Duke, is married to Jane Richard. They have four children. Since inheriting the title Duke Ralph has overseen major changes to Syon park with the removal of architecturally inappropriate modern structures and the building of the Syon Hotel and major restoration works to Syon House and the parkland and historic structures.

# THE PERCY FAMILY AT
# SYON HOUSE

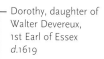

**Henry Percy, K.G.**
9th Earl of Northumberland,
*b.*1564 *d.*1632
(imprisoned in the Tower 1605 - 1622)

Dorothy, daughter of
Walter Devereux,
1st Earl of Essex
*d.*1619

**Algernon Percy, K.G.**
10th Earl of Northumberland,
*b.*1602 *d.*1668

Elizabeth, daughter of
Theophilus Howard,
2nd Earl of Suffolk
*d.*1705

**Josceline Percy**
11th Earl of Northumberland,
*b.*1644 *d.*1670

Elizabeth, daughter of
Thomas Wriotheseley,
4th Earl of Southampton
*d.*1690

**Elizabeth Percy**
*b.*1667 *d.*1722

(1)  Earl of Ogle
(2)  Thomas Thynne
(3)  Charles, 6th Duke of Somerset
      *b.*1662 *d.*1748

**Algernon Seymour**
7th Duke of Somerset, *b.*1684 *d.*1750; created
Earl of Northumberland 1749 with remainder
in default of male heirs to his son-in-law

Frances, daughter of
Hon. Henry Thynne
*d.*1754

**Elizabeth Seymour**
*b.*1716 *d.*1776

Sir Hugh Smithson, K.G. *b.*1714/15 *d.*1786
Succeeded as Earl of Northumberland 1750,
taking the names and arms of Percy; created
1st Duke of Northumberland 1766

**Hugh Percy K.G.**
2nd Duke,
*b.*1742 *d.*1817

Frances, daughter
of Peter Burrell of
Beckenham, Kent
*b.*1752 *d.*1820

Algernon Percy
1st Earl of Beverley
*b.*1750 *d.*1830

Isabella, daughter
of Peter Burrell of
Beckenham, Kent
*d.*1812

**Hugh Percy K.G.**
3rd Duke,
*b.*1785 *d.*1847

Charlotte Florentia,
daughter of Edward
Clive, Earl of Powis
*b.*1787 *d.*1866

**Algernon Percy K.G.**
4th Duke,
*b.*1792 *d.*1865

Eleanor, daughter of
Richard Grosvenor, 2nd
Marquess of Westminster
*b.*1820 *d.*1911

**George Percy**
5th Duke, *b.*1788 *d.*1867

Louisa, daughter of
Hon. James Archibald
Stuart-Wortley Mackenzie
*b.*1781 *d.*1848

**Algernon Percy, K.G.**
6th Duke, *b.*1810 *d.*1899

Louisa, daughter of
Henry Drummond of
Albury Park, Surrey
*b.*1813 *d.*1890

**Henry George Percy, K.G.**
7th Duke, *b.*1846 *d.*1918

Edith, daughter of
George Douglas Campbell
7th Duke of Argyll
*b.*1849 *d.*1913

**Alan Ian Percy, K.G.**
8th Duke, *b.*1880 *d.*1930

Helen, daughter of
Charles Gordon-Lennox
7th Duke of Richmond
*b.*1886 *d.*1965

**Henry George Alan Percy**
9th Duke, *b.*1912 *d.*1940
(killed in action)

**Hugh Algernon Percy, K.G.**
10th Duke, *b.*1914 *d.*1988

Elizabeth, daughter of
8th Duke of Buccleuch
*b.*1922 *d.*2012

**Henry Alan Walter Richard Percy**
11th Duke, *b.*1953 *d.*1995

**Ralph George Algernon Percy**
12th Duke, *b.*1956

Jane, daughter of
John Richard
*b.*1958

# THE HOUSE

# THE GREAT HALL

*The entrance to the Great Hall is through the porte-cochère, built in the 1820s when the exterior walls of the house were refaced with Bath stone by the 3rd Duke.*

Robert Adam's instructions were 'to create a palace of Graeco-Roman splendour', and the Great Hall realises the full grandeur of his skill. Based on a Roman Basilica and probably inspired by the work of Piranesi, work started in 1762 and finished in 1769. Adam was confronted with difficulties in the uneven floor levels of the Tudor house as the Great Hall was above the outside ground levels but below the principal floor level. Adam overcame these problems by the two-armed staircase leading to a tunnel-vaulted recess with Doric columns supporting the entablature which continues around the hall. At the other end of the hall is a shallow step up to the coffered apse, and behind this concealed steps lead to the rest of the house, hidden by curved doors. The apse and recess turn the room into a double cube, and the design of the ceiling is reflected in the pattern of the marble flooring. The Great Hall was repainted in 2007/8 to a colour scheme based on the original Adam design.

Robert Adam (1728-1792).
Courtesy of the National Portrait Gallery, London

There are four large statues representing classical figures standing on Adam-designed pedestals, executed by Joseph Rose. The Hall is dominated at either end by statues of the Dying Gaul and the Apollo Belvedere. The Dying Gaul by Luigi Valadier is a copy of the original in the Capitoline Museum in Rome, and the first Duchess recorded that she paid £300 for the statue. The bronze was cast in Rome and achieved its green patina by being immersed for nine years in brine. The Apollo cost less and was produced quickly, largely because Valadier did not undertake the commission for a bronze Laocoon which was originally to stand in this location.

*The Hall chairs are made from English oak decorated with the Garter surrounding the Percy crest. They were made by Robert Hughes for the 3rd Duke in 1833.*

Some of the busts are antique, notably Demosthenes, 2nd century BCE Roman, Marcus Aurelius 2nd century CE and Antisthenes, this being a 3/4th century BCE head on a much later socle. The antique classical busts include Antisthenes, Socrates, the Emperors Augustus and Marcus Aurelius. The bust of Claudius is an 18th century copy and there are busts in the classical styles of the 1st Duke of Northumberland and William Pitt the younger. The pier table positioned in front of the Dying Gaul was designed by Adam showing an inlay of coloured marble, with typical anthemion design. The high level chiaroscuro circular paintings are by Andrea Casali, with details taken from Constantine's Arch in Rome. They are cleverly painted so that the figures are in proportion when seen from below.

*Marble bust of Socrates.*

# THE ANTE ROOM

*The contrast between the Great Hall and the Ante Room or
Vestibule is startling. Here the vivid colourings are enhanced
by the twelve Ionic columns veneered with verdantique
scagliola, obtained by James Adam in Rome in 1765. The
gilded statues above were executed by John Cheere. This room
was extensively restored in 2000.*

The floor is one of the earliest examples in
Britain of scagliola, a composite of marble,
fixing materials and colouring matter. Wear
to the original floor necessitated repairs in
1832 by William Croggan, and more recent
restoration work has also been carried out.
The ceiling and gilded trophy panels on the
walls are by Joseph Rose. They were inspired
by those in the Villa Madama in Rome and Adam was so pleased with
Rose's work that it is said he paid for them out of his own pocket. The
statuary marble and verdantique chimney piece were carved by
Joseph Wilton to designs by Adam. The Wedgwood plaque above
is a replica in plaster of an antique relief now in the Louvre,
called the New Bride. The two bronze statues are by Valadier.
They are of Silenus with the infant Dionysus and Antinous,
a favourite of Emperor Hadrian.

The design of the Ante Room is highly geometrical,
but relies on the clever arrangement of the columns
as the room is actually rectangular, measuring
11.1 metres by 9.1 metres. The form of a square
is obtained by bringing forward the columns on
one side to stand clear of the wall, supporting the
entablature which continues around the room. The
vertical line is maintained by statues standing upright
over the columns. The room thus gives the effect of
being square with the minimum loss of floor space. The
right hand window, facing the south lawn, has also been
cleverly disguised as a doorway and leads to an external
staircase. The Ante Room was also used as a small
dining room and King William IV was entertained here
in 1832.

*Statue of Mercury.*

# THE DINING ROOM

*The Dining Room was the first of the state rooms to be finished in 1763.*
*Measuring 20.1 metres by 6.5 metres, it is very nearly a triple cube.*

With its arched recesses, apses, half domes and columnar screens, the Dining Room is quintessentially Adam and illustrative of his declared intention to '*parade the conveniences and the social pleasures of life*'. Adam shows great skill in using screens of Corinthian columns before apsidal recesses at each

end, thus hiding ugly square corners. The ceiling plaster is the work of Joseph Rose, and the chiaroscuro frieze panels are by Andrea Casali. The Dining Room is finished in stucco rather than damask or tapestries so that it might not "*retain the smell of the victuals*".

*The chimney piece is by Thomas and Benjamin Carter to a design by Adam. Above is a marble panel of the Three Graces, the daughters of Zeus, by Luc- Francois Breton.*

Joseph Wilton was reportedly paid more than £200 for the copy of Michelangelo's Bacchus, which he made from a cast in the Duke of Richmond's Academy at Whitehall. The statue of Ceres is one of the very few complete statues by Bartolomeo Cavaceppi who was known as 'The Prince of Restorers'. The pier tables are of the early Adam period with the marble tops coming from Italy, the two semi-circular tables by the windows have scagliola tops and all came from Northumberland House. William Collins' gilt brass lamps, decorated with Percy lions at the base on mahogany pedestals by Morel and Hughes, were made for the Great Dining Room of Northumberland House in 1824.

*The clock in the corner of the room is of English manufacture of about 1785 by the renowned Swiss clockmaker, Benjamin Vulliamy. The pedestal contains musical pipes which play various tunes. It is overlaid with scagliola and painted in the centre with an oval monochrome medallion of Apollo driving the chariot of the sun, from a design by Cipriani, executed by John Bronnley, coach painter to George III.*

*A Muse of Music, Apollo and Flora.*

# THE RED DRAWING ROOM

*Adam intended the Red Drawing Room to serve as an Ante Room to the real Withdrawing or Ladies' Room - The Long Gallery. He explained that his reason for making the Gallery the Ladies' Drawing Room was that they should not be disturbed by sounds of revelry emerging from the Dining Room.*

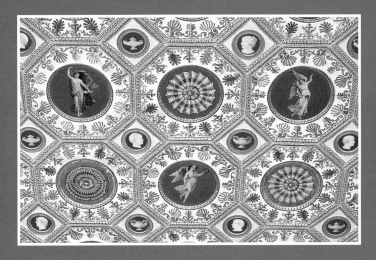

The Drawing Room is in vivid contrast to the subtle colour scheme of the Dining Room. The wall hangings of cerise Spitalfield silk were probably re-woven in the 1820s and were reversed and re-hung following conservation work carried out in 1965. The coved ceiling, inspired by work in the Villa Madama, Rome, was executed by Joseph Rose. The 239 medallions decorating the ceiling are by Cipriani and depict Arcadian figures. They were indirectly referred to by Adam's rival architect, Sir William Chambers, as resembling 'skied dinner plates'. In the 75 central medallions the figures are floating in the heavens, whilst those around the edge are sitting or standing on solid ground.

*18th century mosaic table.*

*The ormolu used extensively around the doorways and chimney piece is achieved by gilding a metal alloy ~ examples of some of the superb craftsmanship to be found in the Red Drawing Room.*

Thomas Moore, of Moorfields in London, manufactured the carpet in 1769 to a design by Adam. The Greek honeysuckle pattern in the carpet border is repeated around the ceiling medallions, across the fireplace, and on other main features in the room. The white marble chimney piece is by Thomas and Benjamin Carter to a design by Adam. The doorways are remarkable for the ivory background of the pilaster panels which are filled in with ormolu medallions. The pier tables in front of the mirrors were designed by Adam and made in Italy. The small mosaic table under Elizabeth of Bohemia is said to be from the Baths of Titus in Rome, and was procured by James Adam in 1765. The mirrors are particularly fine examples of very large sheet glass extending right down to the pier tables. The frames were designed by Adam, with later additions. There was an attempt to evade the punitive import duty on the mirrors by asking the Venetian ambassador to bring them in his diplomatic luggage. This was unsuccessful, and the duty was paid.

*The Red Drawing Room during the early part of the 20th century.*

Elizabeth, Queen of Bohemia by Van Miereveldt. Elizabeth was the sister of King Charles I and married King Fredrick V, the Elector Palatine. Known as the "Winter Queen", she was the grandmother of the future King George I of England. Her third son was Prince Rupert, the flamboyant Cavalier Soldier who fought at the Battle of Brentford in 1642.

Henrietta, Duchess of Orleans, by Mignard, youngest daughter of King Charles I and known as 'Minette'. She arranged the secret treaty of Dover in 1670 between King Charles II and King Louis XIV of France, less than a month before her death at the age of 26.

Princess Mary of Orange, by Adriaen Hanneman. The eldest daughter of King Charles I she married William, Prince of Orange, and her son became William III of England.

Queen Henrietta Maria of France, the wife of King Charles I and mother of Charles II and James II.

# THE LONG GALLERY

*The Long Gallery was planned by Adam for the particular delight of the ladies: 'finished in a style to afford variety and amusement'. Measuring 41.4 metres by 4.2 metres its length is ten times the width and takes up the whole of the east front, standing over the colonnade.*

The Long Gallery was planned by Adam for the particular delight of the ladies: 'finished in a style to afford variety and amusement'. Measuring 41.4 metres by 4.2 metres its length is ten times the width and takes up the whole of the east front, standing over the colonnade. The room is the former Tudor Long Gallery and more than any other reflects the true genius of Adam. He transformed the once panelled gallery by dividing the wall opposite the eleven windows into five bays centred on three doors and two fireplaces, divided by groups of four pilasters comprising book shelves at wide intervals. By taking the sixty-two Corinthian pilasters with inserts painted by Michelangelo Pergolesi up to the ceiling he suggested height and by his use of the diagonals in the ceiling he gave an impression of width. On entering the Gallery from the Red Drawing Room, a false bookcase on the right is a concealed door leading to steps to the south lawn. The stucco duro roundels are by Joseph Wilton. The carpet incorporates in its borders the original design by Pergolesi of 1765 and was made in 1967 by the Royal Wilton Carpet Company. The library contains more than 3,000 books. At each end of the Gallery are small boudoirs or closets known as the turret rooms. The one at the south-east end is square and hung with silk and mirrors painted by the 3rd

Duchess and added to by Ponsonby. The Turret Room at the north-east end is exquisitely decorated in stucco with a design of a rich classical composition. Hanging from the domed ceiling is a late 18th century mechanical singing bird with a timepiece.

Much of the furniture is contemporary with the Adam period c. 1765-1775, including the pair of sofas and set of armchairs covered in needlework which came from the Tapestry Room of Northumberland House. These were supposedly reworked by French emigres living at Orleans House c. 1790 to an Elizabethan tent stitch design. Above the fireplaces are lunettes by Francesco Zuccarelli, a founder member of the Royal Academy. The portrait medallions around the Gallery show the lineage of the Percy family, which claims descent from Charlemagne, the first Emperor of the Holy Roman Empire.

The portraits up to, and possibly including, that of the 2nd Duke are by Francis Lindo, a local Isleworth artist. Looking out of the windows at the views across the tidal water meadows of the River Thames towards Kew Gardens, it is hard to imagine that one is only a few miles from central London.

*Proposed design for the Long Gallery by Robert Adam.*
Courtesy, the board of Trustees of the Victoria and Albert Museum.

# THE PRINT ROOM

*In 1824 the 3rd Duke paid Thomas Ponsonby and his men to remove one hundred prints and their borders from the walls, but the room has retained its name until the present day. The 1st Duchess of Northumberland was a great collector of prints which she bought in large quantities while travelling the Continent.*

The Print Room forms part of the alterations to the north side of the house, carried out by the 3rd Duke in the 1820s. The ceiling was created in 1863 to a design by Giovanni Montiroli, who also designed many rooms at Alnwick Castle in the style of the Italian Renaissance. When the house opened to the public in 1951 the 10th Duke placed various pieces of 18th century English bedroom furniture here for the 'general interest of the visitors'.

Portraits of some of those who formed the history of Syon are displayed in this room. Those relating to Syon's Tudor history hang near the Long Gallery door, including Edward Seymour, Duke of Somerset, who built Syon House in the 1540s. Others are predominantly seventeenth and eighteenth century, including the ninth Earl of Northumberland who acquired Syon House through marriage in 1594.

Major John Norton, painted by Thomas Phillips, was a Scottish soldier of Cherokee descent. He was known as Chief Teyoninhokarawen and his 'journey of 1000 miles down the Ohio', written in 1809, was dedicated to Hugh, 2nd Duke of Northumberland, who fought in the American War of Independence.

George III rosewood and parcel-gilt mosaic table supplied by Morel and Hughes in 1825 representing Bacchaus.

James Smithson (1765 – 1829) was the natural son of the 1st Duke of Northumberland and Elizabeth Macie. On his death in 1829 his will stated that in the absence of descendants, his money should be left to 'The United States of America, to found at Washington, under the name of the Smithsonian Institute, an establishment for the increase and diffusion of knowledge among men'. The bequest was paid in gold sovereigns and delivered to the United States mint in Philadelphia, where it was valued in excess of half a million dollars the equivalent of more than $75,000,000 in modern money.

A Carrara marble and granite chimney piece, circa 1750, from Northumberland House.

# THE DUCHESS' SITTING ROOM

*Although much altered, this room forms part of the inner suite of family rooms dating back to the 16th century and is shown on Robert Adam's plan of the house as a bedchamber. More recently it has been used as a family sitting room.*

The marble fireplace, with its carved plaque representing Aesop's Fable of the Fox and the Stork, was brought from Northumberland House. The two 18th century armchairs in front of it have tapestry covers stitched by Helen, 8th Duchess, and her sister in the 1930s. Other 18th century pieces here include the bow-front satinwood commode and the mahogany display cabinet by Vile, both against the wall to the left, and the Queen Anne walnut bureau cabinet on the right. The concertina-action George II card table, on which the

chess set is displayed, is one of a pair and the unusual two-tier table was originally two stools and is also part of a set. This dates from the early 19th century, as does the impressive calamander wood library writing table in the centre of the room. Both were made by Morel and Hughes for Northumberland House.

Much of the porcelain is 18th century, both European and Oriental, and the paintings are mainly Dutch, collected by the 1st Duchess.

# THE GREEN DRAWING ROOM

*The Green Drawing Room is still regularly used by the family. The ornate Renaissance-style ceiling, as in the Print Room and Dining Room, was designed by Giovanni Montiroli and executed by Charles Smith in 1863-4.*

The superb scagliola fireplace, designed by Adam for the Glass Drawing Room of Northumberland House, was installed in 1924. The grate is made of paktong, an alloy of copper, nickel and zinc which does not tarnish. Much of the furniture is 18th century, including the suite of beech wood furniture, the two marquetry serpentine commodes standing either side of the fireplace, and the Italian topped micro-mosaic gilt wood side tables on the left hand side of the room. The chandelier is English and dates from the 1830s.

The paintings include portraits of King Edward VI as an infant above the fireplace, studio of Holbein, and Andrew Drummond by Sir Joshua Reynolds above the piano.

# THE PRIVATE DINING ROOM

*This room has been used as a private dining room since Robert Adam remodelled the house.*

*The spectacular gilt-brass waterfall chandelier made by William Collins dates from about 1825 and was made for the Glass Drawing Room of Northumberland House. It is designed as a fountain, with three entwined dolphins spouting jets of water and hung with glass beads depicting droplets of water.*

Much of the furniture here dates from the early 19th century and was supplied for this room by Robert Hughes. This includes the mahogany extending table, the dining chairs, the two large sideboards with cellarets or wine coolers and the two marble-topped tables. Dating from about 1770 are the two mahogany pedestals, with lidded leaf carved cisterns, standing at each end of the sideboard at the far end of the room. Displayed on the sideboards and table are pieces of gilded French porcelain from the Paris Dagoty dessert service, purchased by the 3rd Duke in the 1820s. Outstanding among the portraits are those of the 1st Duke, by James Barry, and his Duchess, after Sir Joshua Reynolds, over the sideboards. The charming family group of the 2nd Duke's children, painted by Gilbert Stuart at Syon in the summer of 1787 hangs above the fireplace.

# THE OAK PASSAGE

*The passage is another of the 3rd Duke's additions constructed during the 1820s to provide a service corridor. Today it contains many interesting royal and family portraits. The interior wall is part of the outer wall of the original house.*

The wainscot panelling probably dates from the early 16th century and it is thought that these panels came from Leconfield, a former Percy residence in Yorkshire, and were brought to Syon by the 9th Earl. They may have originally been painted in the Percy colours of blue and gold (top right). The 1635 Moses Glover map of the "Istelworth Hundred and the Mannor at Sion", and Jan Griffier's painting of Syon and its surroundings are of particular interest, as both show the formal landscape of Syon of the seventeenth and early eighteenth centuries.

*The wainscot panelling, digitally altered to show how it may have looked in the early 16th century.*

*A copy of Canaletto's painting of Syon in 1749 (now on display at Alnwick Castle). Sir Hugh Smithson (later the 1st Duke) recorded 'Mr Canaletti has begun the picture of Syon and by the outlines upon the canvas I think it will have a noble effect'. This painting shows how the formal gardens towards the river had been cleared by 1749.*

*Arthur, Prince of Wales, eldest son of Henry VII. Died 1502 at the age of 15.*

# NORTHUMBERLAND HOUSE

*Northumberland House was the family's principal London residence.*

*Canaletto's painting of Northumberland House (now on display at Alnwick Castle), clearly shows the statant lion, after a model by Michelangelo, which was removed to Syon where it can be seen today on the east front of the house.*

Built in 1605 for the Earl of Northampton, the house came to the Percy family in 1642 on the 10th Earl of Northumberland's marriage to Elizabeth Howard, daughter of the Earl of Suffolk, and was renamed Northumberland House. The house had 150 private rooms for the family as well as the usual service rooms and extended from the Strand to the river. When demolished by the Metropolitan Board of Works in 1874, Northumberland House was the last of London's great private riverside palaces.

The oar near the portrait of William Timms is from the Duke's state barge. The River Thames was a principal thoroughfare for noblemen travelling to and from their houses or attending court and the 1st Duke and Duchess would journey between Northumberland House and Syon for an evening's entertainment.

William Timms was 95 years old in 1838 when this portrait was painted by Emma Soyer. He served three sovereigns and three Dukes of Northumberland as waterman.

# THE PRINCIPAL STAIRCASE

*Leading off the West Corridor is the principal staircase. In the well can be seen the Sèvres vase given by the French King Charles X to the 3rd Duke, who attended his coronation in 1825 as Great Britain's Ambassador Extraordinary.*

Near the vase is a sedan chair, bearing the arms of the 1st Duke. On the wall is the painting Diana returning from the Hunt, attributed to the studio of Rubens and de Vos. The West Corridor leads back into the Great Hall, and so ends what Sir John Betjeman described as 'The Grand Architectural Walk'.

'Diana returning from the Hunt' attributed to the studio of Rubens and de Vos.

# THE UPPER FLOOR

*An inventory carried out in 1847 at the time of the 3rd Duke's death gives a detailed description of every room in the house and the present-day layout reflects the remodelling undertaken during the 1820s and 1830s.*

The main staircase leads to the landing along the North Front or the Nursery Passage and to the Pink and Blue bedrooms, with their adjoining dressing rooms, furnished in the style of the 1900s. The present Duke and his brothers and sisters occupied these rooms as children when the family visited Syon each year during the late spring and early summer. The Pink bedroom was their nursery dayroom.

The Duchess of Kent's bedroom.

*Bedrooms along the Nursery Passage.*

# THE EAST FRONT

*This wing contains the principal suite of State bedrooms, furnished by Robert Hughes in 1832 for the use of the young Princess Victoria (below), and her mother, the Duchess of Kent.*

Charlotte Florentia, the 3rd Duchess, was the official governess of the young Princess Victoria, who regularly stayed at Syon. The gilt wood four poster bed in the Duchess of Kent's room dates from 1790 but was substantially altered by Hughes, who also supplied a new 'Polonese Bedstead' for the Princess in her bedroom (opposite). Each bed had three mattresses: the lower one of straw, the second of horsehair or wool, and the top layer, known as the bed rather than a mattress, filled with chicken or goose feathers. Hughes also supplied a feather bolster and two down pillows, three 'superfine' Witney blankets and a Marseilles quilt for each bed.

*Portrait of Princess Victoria of Kent (1819-1901), later Queen Victoria by George Hayter (1792-1871).*

# THE HOUSEHOLD AND ENTERTAINING

*Syon has throughout the centuries hosted some lavish parties since the 9th Earl entertained King James I in 1603. This banquet cost the equivalent of £20,000 in today's money, of which more than £6,000 was spent on wine. The household consumed enormous amounts of food and drink. In the 10th Earl's time, for example, an annual account records that 200 barrels of beer, 4,197 dozen loaves and 18 cakes, plus a parmesan wedge weighing 35lbs were purchased for his lordship's table.*

> 118
>
> *Housemaids*
>
> 1 They are never to go out without leave from the Housekeeper
>
> 2 They are always to keep themselves clean & neat but not to dress above their station

In the mid-18th century the 1st Duchess employed 50 servants and was keen to practise economy in her household. She made the calculation that a servant would eat a pound of meat, half a pound of potatoes, a loaf of bread and two pints of beer a day, at a total cost of no more than 8 pence each. She was also very particular in the way she expected the servants to behave when at Syon and she drew up a set of rules for the Servants' Hall. At the beginning of the 19th century, a detailed set of 'Regulations' replaced these rules. The 2nd Duke, a military man, liked to order his household as if he was in command of a regiment, and a clear distinction was drawn between the upper-servants and those who performed the more mundane duties.

## *HOURS TO BE OBSERVED*

> *Hours to be observ'd* — 119
>
> | | |
> |---|---|
> | Prayers Tuesdays & Fridays | 9 |
> | Breakfast | 10 |
> | Church on Sundays | 10¾ |
> | Airing | 11 |
> | Dinner | 4 |
> | Coffee | 5½ |
> | Tea | 7¾ |
> | Supper | 10½ |
> | Summons to Bed | 12 |

*SERVANTS' HALL*

> 256
>
> *Servants Hall*
>
> 1 No swearing cursing or indecent Language is to be suffer'd at the Servants Table & any person guilty of it is for the first fault to be turn'd out of the Servants Hall, and not to be re admitted but upon asking pardon & promising to behave better for the future & if they repeat the fault they shall be turn'd away
>
> 2 No Servant is allow'd to quarrel or give ill Language to another
>
> 3 Any Servant who strikes another shall be immediately discharged
>
> 4 Breakfast is to be set upon Servants Hall Table at 9 & so to continue till 10 When the Usher of the Hall is to carry it back again to the Kitchen and it is to be set on the Table when their Bell rings & Servants must be all out of the Servants Hall again in less than 2 Hours from that Time & at Night when the Bell rings for the Duke & Duchess to go to Bed, all the Servts are to quit the Servants Hall without delay or disturbance
>
> 5 The Servants Breakfast is to continue upon the Table

The Duke demanded the very highest service and exemplary behaviour from his upper-servants expecting them to be a shining example to those whom they controlled. He regarded the whole household of servants as part of the 'family' for whom he was personally responsible and a servant could only be dismissed from the household on his personal command.

*The Confectioner's Kitchen c. 1830.*

The upper-servants included the Steward of the Household, the Valet de Chambre, the Groom of the Chambers and the Butler – each of whom had specific duties in the smooth running of the household. This was under the overall control of the Steward, while the Groom looked after the apartments and saw to it that the servants were well turned out. The Valet's duties were personal to the family and the Butler had charge of the silverware and the wine cellar.

Much of the economy of the household, as well as the social prestige of the family, rested on the kitchen, where there were three principal servants - the Clerk of the Kitchen who ordered the food supplies, the Cook who created the menu and oversaw the daily working of the kitchen and the Confectioner, who was the specialist purveyor of the sorbets, ices and jellies which graced the tables when the Duke and Duchess entertained. According to the figures given in the Clerk of Kitchen's lists in the first fortnight in August 1820, the household consumed 578lbs of beef, 225lbs of mutton and 144lbs of veal as well as 25 head of poultry and rabbits. In addition 260 eggs and 31lbs of butter together with 3 pecks of flour, 52 loaves and 7 ¼ lbs of tea were provided.

An inventory of the house at the time of the 3rd Duke's death in 1847 provides a full description of the basement of the house. The basement contained staff quarters, including the Steward's Room for the upper servants and the Servants' Hall for the rest. The Confectionery was a major department of the household and the Confectioner had his own bedroom, complete with chintz curtains, Brussels carpet, bed with hair mattress and a mahogany table. The Confectioner also had his own cellar below stairs, with preserving pans, stewing stoves, sieves and steamers and 10 pewter freezing pots. The bedrooms of the Clerk of the Kitchens and the Cook were attached to the kitchen area on the north side of the house. The kitchen itself contained a range, spits, stewing stoves and a whole range of copper and tin equipment including 83 stew pans, coppers for baking, sauce pans, small kettles and a fish kettle large enough to take a turbot.

The basement also contained the Secretary's room, the Housekeeper's room and the Valet de Chambre's bedroom, together with the sleeping quarters for eight footman and male servants. The laundry maids had their own quarters alongside the laundry and wash house and the postillions and coachmen were housed in the stable block along with the Master of Horse. There was also a separate sick bay for servants who fell ill.

*These cut-away drawings by Peter Brears are conjectural and are based on inventories taken in 1632 and 1847.*

## The house depicted at the time of the 9th Earl's death.

*The principal room on the west front was the Hall. The Long Gallery ran the length of the east front. The south front contained the Dining Room, the Withdrawing Chamber and three bedrooms. The attached brick building on the north side housed the kitchen range and the corresponding building on the south side, lodgings.*

## The house depicted at the time of the 3rd Duke's death.

*The rooms on the principal floor follow a similar layout as today. The main difference is the kitchen range to the north which is now garages and staff accommodation.*

## The vaulted undercroft below the Great Hall was used as the Confectioner's cellar with the Confectionery, located below the Ante Room.

*The Butler's plate pantry and servants' bedrooms occupied the remainder of the south front. Further servants' bedrooms were on the east side of the house behind the colonnade. The Steward's Room and Servant's Hall were on the north side, with the Housekeeper's room situated at the end of the passage facing west.*

Annual Wages in 1845:

Cook (Louis Limousin) .................................... £150

Confectioner .................................................... £110

Footmen ......................................................... £28

Laundry Maids ................................................ £14

Total Salary Bill ............................................. £753

Throughout the Victorian era and much of the 20th century, Syon was used as a summer residence by the family, and the Royal Family and other distinguished guests were often entertained.

*'More than one hundred tenants sat down to dinner in the Great Hall. The delicacies of the season and rare wines from the old cellars of the Mansion heightened the enjoyment of the feast which was furnished with the traditional Barons of Beef, and the Band of the Grenadier Guards gave the company some delightful music'.*

*Account of a banquet given by the 5th Duke in 1867*

### SYON.

DÉJEUNER DU 15 JUILLET, 1886.

## MENU.

Pâté chaud froid de Cailles.
Galantine de Volaille.
Jambon à l'Aspic.
Bœuf à l'Ecarlate.
Petits Aspics à la Cardinal.
Profitrolles à l'Indienne.
Profitrolles à la Reine.
Chaud froid de Volaille.
Chaud froid de Cailles Truffés.
Poulets rôtis.
Jambon.
Langue de Bœuf.
Sandwiches—Volaille, Jambon, Langue, Strasbourg.
Babas.
Gelées.
Crèmes.
Macedoine de Fruits.
Pâtisseries.
Gateaux.

*A 19th century menu from one of Syon House's banquets.*

*A Victorian garden party at Syon.*

# THE GARDENS

*The gardens at Syon Park contain elements from several historic periods but are continually changing, both over the years and through the seasons.*

The first gardens at Syon would have been associated with the abbey which was, by this time, a huge and sprawling complex centred on the church. Plants would have been grown both for food and medicinal purposes. Thomas Betson, librarian of Syon Abbey, published his herbal at Syon in the early sixteenth century, and listed many plants which would have been grown at the abbey, and listed their uses. A generation later there was a heated argument between one of Henry VIII's agents, Thomas Bedyll, and a priest of Syon Richard Whitford in the abbey gardens.

*"I hameried Whitford in the garden bothe with faire wordes and with foule.......but he hath a brasyn forehed, which shameth at nothing..."*
From Sion the xviith day of December, Thomas Bedyll.

*A detail from The Tresswell Map of 1607.*

In 1547 the lease of Syon passed to Edward Seymour, Duke of Somerset, who demolished the remaining abbey buildings to create a grand new riverside palace. Between house and river Somerset's physician, the botanist William Turner, laid out what has been called the first botanic garden in Britain, a formal garden in the latest Italian style, probably based on geometric forms, with avenues and terraces. In later years, Turner recalled meeting the young Princess Elizabeth at Syon, and conversing with her in Latin, which she spoke better than any woman he had met on all his travels. It was also at Syon in 1548 that Turner wrote *The Names of Herbes* listing many plants growing both in the gardens of Syon and the surrounding countryside. Turner was an extremely influential naturalist, writing works on ornithology, fish and plants, and has been called "The Father of English Botany".

Much of his work was based on his own personal researches, but he was especially notable as the first scientific writer to produce his works in the English language, allowing them to be accessible to any literate person, rather than remaining the exclusive domain of doctors and apothecaries.

The earliest plan of the landscape surrounding Syon house is the Treswell map of 1607. This shows Syon House in the time of the 9th Earl. There are orchards to the north, fields to the west, and the outline of formal gardens to the south and east.

The Treswell map was essentially about recording field boundaries and landholdings, and so the details of the ornamental gardens are omitted. However, in 1635 the cartographer Moses Glover produced another map, in which these details are clearly seen. There is a triangular terrace to the south east overlooking the river and a large parterre centred on the north east corner of Syon House. The service buildings are all to the north, on the site presently occupied by the Garden Centre, but the area outside the Pepperpot lodges is laid out as farmland as far as the London Road.

Algernon, the 10th Earl, shared his father's interest in horticulture and participated in the great tulip speculation known as 'Tulipmania', spending huge sums on imported bulbs before the market crashed in 1634. By the early 17th century, the lead in garden design had moved from Italy to France, and Algernon employed a French gardener to lay out a new garden to the south of Syon House, centred on a great fountain. The French gardens of the time were very formal, and the new garden at Syon was one of the first examples of this style in the country, with parterres and allées of lime and cypress.

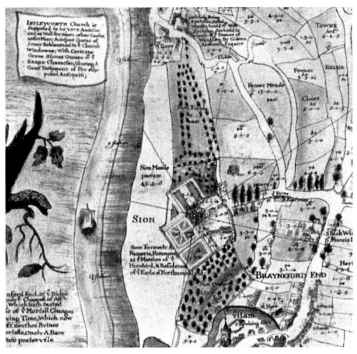

*A detail from Moses Glover's 1635 map showing Syon (Sion) House.*

Over the next century, the formal grounds around Syon House continued to develop. The great Lime Avenue leading to the west gates was laid out at this time, as were a series of further avenues, probably of lime. The Fairchild plan of 1741 shows the designed gardens stretching into the wider landscape, but indicates that there had been considerable damage as a result of a period of frost and drought, both especially destructive to the evergreens which would have provided the framework of the design.

At the same time, this style of gardening was rapidly going out of fashion. All was to change in the second half of the eighteenth century, as the works inside the house were mirrored in the grounds and Syon was described as 'one of the finest villas in Europe'. The removal of the formal gardens between House and river had been started before 1749, but, over a period of some twenty years, Lancelot 'Capability' Brown took this work much further, creating a park from surrounding farmland, diverting the old road from Isleworth to Brentford, demolishing various farm buildings and taking advantage of the damp fields along the line

of the prehistoric channel of the Thames to excavate two new lakes. Trees were essential to Brown's style, and suitably sited specimens and clumps, including some that are still standing, were retained, and a huge number of new specimens planted. To the north of Syon House orchards and vegetable gardens were re-located to an improved and enlarged site and Brown created 'Syon Pleasure Ground', centred on the Inner Lake, with trees and walks, boasting 'every foreign shrub, plant and flower which may be adopted by the soil of this climate', and 'the choicest trees and plants from all quarters of the globe' as well as the statue of the goddess Flora on a 55 foot Doric column which stands to the north of Syon House. The new 'productive' gardens also gave an opportunity to increase the range of crops grown: a hot wall was built for the growing of vines, new melon pits were dug, and stove houses built for the cultivation of pineapples. It would have been in one of these buildings that the first tea plant to grow in Europe flowered in 1773. In 1764, George III commissioned Brown to landscape the grounds of his palace, on the site which is now Kew Gardens. While Brown's work at Kew is concealed by later developments, this was unique as the only example of adjacent Brown landscapes, with the river as the centrepiece rather than the dividing line.

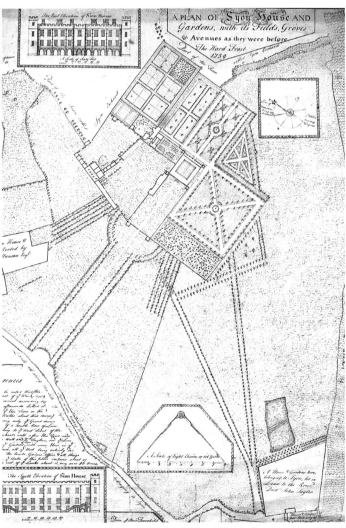

*A plan of Syon House and Gardens before the Hard Frost of 1739, by Christopher Fairchild.*

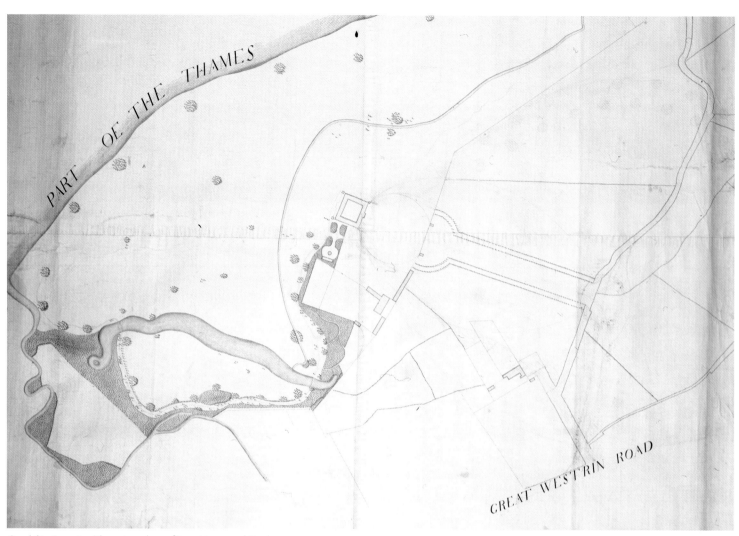

*Capability Brown's 18th century plans of Syon House and Gardens.*

The centrepiece of the gardens is the Great Conservatory, one of the finest garden structures in the country. The Great Conservatory was built between 1826 and 1827 to the rear of the old botanic house, which was sensibly preserved until the peach crop of 1827 had ripened. The masonry work was undertaken in Bath stone by Thomas Cundy, and the metalwork and furnaces by the garden engineering specialists James Wright Richards of Birmingham.

The architect of this remarkable building was Charles Fowler, co-founder of the Institute of British Architects and designer of the covered market at Covent Garden. At Syon, Fowler also designed the Riding School with its remarkable iron truss roof and the clock tower on the stable block. What Fowler constructed in the gardens has been described as a conservatory in a transitional style, a cross between the 18th century orangery and a Victorian conservatory. The inspiration for the layout of the conservatory was again classical, as Fowler turned to the works of Palladio and took as his model the unfinished villa of the Counts Lodovico and Francesco Trissino at Meledo. Whilst the villa was centred on a classic dome, Fowler applied the new theories of curvilinear greenhouses to create a glass dome surmounted by a cupola, which was as technologically advanced as it was architecturally

innovative, with pillars and trusses constructed of cast iron but with the ribs of the dome made of wrought iron. This design of building permitted high levels of natural light, complemented by an elaborate and advanced heating system, with four miles of piping. Letters show that the Duke took a close interest in the smallest technical detail of the construction, and insisted on being kept informed of any changes or problems that occurred. The Duke sent a strongly worded letter to Head Gardener Richard Forrest when the project showed signs of running over budget.

*"Forrest,*
*You will give an immediate order that no more stone*
*will be forwarded to you for the rockery until I have*
*decided what will be wanted and have given you an*
*order in writing....the whole of the labourers employed*
*about the Rockery and Botanical Garden are to be paid*
*off tomorrow. I desire also that you will make out an*
*abstract of the whole of your accounts since you have*
*been at Syon explanatory of the different branches*
*of the expenditure and also let me have a list of all*
*persons employed since the end of June at Syon and*
*stating how they have been employed..."*

Charles Fowler consulted Richard Forrest about planting and divided the building into a number of separate sections, including plants from Australia, fynbos plants from the tip of South Africa, and small stove (tropical) plants, before opening into the main dome which was planted as a tropical house with palms and giant bamboo in beds and planters. The east wing held a collection of African geraniums (pelargoniums), before another section for heaths, and finally staging for camellias from India and China.

The plants grown in the Great Conservatory were often the latest discoveries from what was then the edge of the known world. The early 19th century was a time of great commercial and imperial expansion, and plants came to Syon by the box-load, from the Cape of Good Hope, West Africa, the West Indies, Australia, South America, India and the South Seas. Despatches from the Botanical gardens at Calcutta included orchids from Nepal and pine seeds from the Himalayas, and the Duke even sent his own ship across the world to collect specimens. Richard Forrest published his Alphabetical Catalogue of Plants of Syon Garden in 1831, and listed over 3,000 species of trees and plants, of which 700 were hardy trees and shrubs, more than 1,000 hardy herbaceous plants, and over 1,500 glasshouse or tropical plants. Grape vines from Syon were sent out to Australia at this time, where they laid the foundations of the country's wine industry. Fifteen botanical gardeners worked in the Great Conservatory and the huge range of service glasshouses behind the scenes.

Today the central dome contains a number of specimen plants in specially commissioned hardwood planters, and the wings are planted with a variety of shrubs and flowers to give an exotic effect. The wings lead to two pavilions, the Cactus House to the east and the Water Lily House to the west. While the Great Conservatory is now completely unheated throughout the year, it does provide some degree of protection which enables the cultivation of less hardy plants.

Beyond the Great Conservatory, lies the lake, or Serpentine River. It was 'Capability' Brown's intention that this should appear to be a completely natural stretch of water, and it forms the centrepiece of the Pleasure Grounds. The walk alongside the lake takes the visitor past some of Syon's finest trees to Flora's Lawn, dominated by a statue of Flora, Goddess of flowers, atop a 55ft Doric column. While the column has stood since the mid-18th century, the original statue of Flora fell in the 20th century and was replaced by a modern replica in 1968 which was struck by lightning a day later, leading to hasty repairs. The banks around the east end of the lake were built up to prevent the regular tidal flooding which previously occurred, and the resulting poor soil provides suitable conditions for a variety of wildflowers. This area is at its best in midsummer, when it is full of butterflies and other insects. The path then leads through the Duke's private woodland, which contains more fine specimen trees, including some of the largest swamp cypresses, Taxodium distichum, in the country.

To the south of Syon House can be found the Wilderness, planted in the late 18th century with the new plants arriving from North America. Today, open lawns with fine specimen trees run to the south. The ha-ha runs along the east of this area, and superbly serves its function as a concealed barrier to the cattle grazing in tide meadow. There are views across the meadow to King George III's Royal Observatory in the Richmond Old Deer Park, and along the Syon Vista to the Palm House in Kew Gardens.

# THE PARK AND ECOLOGY

*The fields and parkland surrounding Syon House cover around 50 hectares, and are of considerable importance in their own right. Although long since surrounded by the spread of London, the park preserves a rural quality and is a haven for a wide variety of wildlife.*

Quércus rùbra.

The red-*leaved*, or *Champion*, Oak.

Courtesy of The Royal Horticultural Society.

From a full-grown tree at Syon, 57 ft. high; diam. of the head, 55 ft. [Scale 1 in. to 12 ft.]

The 1749 Canaletto in the Oak Passage shows cattle grazing in the fields around Syon House, and the fields at Syon are still grazed today. Large areas of the park have been managed in the same way for generations, and this continuity is central to the ecology of the estate. One example is the front lawn, to the west of Syon House, which has been kept as some form of lawn or mown grass since the 16th century. This continuity has led to a

distinctive community of plants and fungi, some extremely rare, the lawn effectively forming a historical artefact as old as the house. The antiquity of the buildings and landscape have allowed a remarkable number of fungi to flourish, with more than 140 species recorded, as well as more than 50 species of lichen.

Although the parkland was landscaped by 'Capability' Brown in the mid-18th century, it was his practice to preserve features from older landscapes, and several trees date from a time when this area was open farmland. The older trees at Syon are valued for the central place they play in the parkland ecosystem, and the habitats they provide, as well as for their antiquity.

Grasslands are particularly important for the conservation of invertebrates. The meadow between Syon House and the river is managed as a traditional hay meadow, and is alive with butterflies, bees, and other insects in the summer. The presence of the insects attracts those species that feed upon them, smaller birds appreciate the shelter and diversity of the gardens, and these in turn attract the attentions of the resident birds of prey. At Syon, around 400 different tree species and many more shrubs and flowers mean that there is shelter and food over much of the year, with no shortage of nesting sites. Syon is fortunate in its proximity to the Thames and for having a long and sheltered lake, containing good numbers of fish which in turn attract grey herons and cormorants. More exotic inhabitants include red-eared terrapins, and ring-necked parakeets: unmistakable, vivid green birds, swooping through the trees in noisy flocks.

A'lnus glutinōsa laciniāta. The cut-leaved glutinous Alder.

Full-grown tree at Syon, 63 ft. high.
[Scale 1 in. to 12 ft.]

The Tide Meadow, designated a Site of Special Scientific Interest, is an area of tidal grassland containing the only significant stretch of natural river bank remaining on the tidal Thames, is truly unique. Large parts of the meadow are flooded twice a day at high tide, and while relatively dry near the ha-ha, it becomes wetter towards the river, where it is intersected by a network of pools, creeks and gullies. The Thames is one of the cleanest metropolitan rivers in the world, supporting more than 130 species of fish and 350 species of invertebrates, and an important breeding site for North Sea fish, ranging from sea bass to plaice. The tide meadow is also notable as one of the few habitats of the rare German hairy snail (Perforatella rubiginosa). Although the tide meadow was planted with clumps of trees in the 18th and 19th centuries, the continuous belt of trees along the riverside is relatively modern, having largely colonised over the last 50 years. In recent years a series of vistas have been cut through this belt of trees to allow views through to the river and to Kew Gardens and the Royal Observatory.

*Harvest time during the First World War.*

# THE HOME FARM AND DAIRY HOUSE

*There was a working farm within Syon Park until the farm buildings were converted for the Gardening Centre in the 1960s. The first farm at Syon would have been established by the Bridgettines for the abbey. It is probable that a section of walling in the much altered monastery barn in the Garden Centre may date from the 16th century.*

During the reign of the 2nd Duke farming became an integral part of Syon activity. The farm was intended to serve the economy of the ducal household at both Syon and Northumberland House.

*HM Queen Elizabeth the Queen Mother, who opened the Garden Centre on the 12th June 1968.*

*The monastery barn at the beginning of the 20th century.*

The 4th Duke had a herd of two dozen Jersey cattle brought from his Stanwick estate. He also added a herd of Highland cattle to add a romantic look to the park. By the second half of the 19th century a flock of Southdown sheep grazed the parkland. Hounslow fair was a popular market for sales, and the visitor centre was the slaughter yard!

An ice house was in use at Syon by 1760-1761, when it is recorded it took twelve men two days to fill it with ice from the lake.

P. Brears

A new ice-house, between the house and the Great Conservatory, was built during the 1820s with two connecting chambers, where ice could survive through the summer months. The ice was used by the Confectioner whose chief duty was to provide the Duke's table with ice cream, sorbets or cool drinks. A dairy house built in 1797-1799, provided a full range of practical facilities, including

lodgings for the dairy maid. After the accession of the 4th Duke, in 1847, it was extended by building the present dairy, attributed to a design by Decimus Burton. Every detail was carefully planned with marble benches, shelves and balustrades, and a fine floor of colourful encaustic tiles. The Duke and his guests could enjoy visits to this elegant dairy, entering it from the Great Conservatory, while the dairy maid continued to carry out most of the practical work in the older dairy nearby. The four plaster panels set into the

*One of the four plaster panels by Joseph Gott, in the dairy house.*

walls of the dairy show infant boys (putti) milking goats, racing greyhounds and harvesting grapes. The 4th Duke commissioned them from Joseph Gott (1786-1860), a leading portrait and animal sculptor who had worked in Rome since 1822. With their playful figures, imaginative design and skilful modelling, they represent some of his finest work.

*A detail from Gott's panel of infant boys milking goats.*

# HOSPITALITY AND EVENTS AT SYON

*"So as to accommodate to the manners of different nations" was one of the key aims of Robert Adam, when remodelling the interior of Syon House for the 1st Duke of Northumberland. Syon was intended for leisure, pleasure and entertaining.*

The desire to entertain guests fashionably on a lavish scale is as relevant today as it was in the 1760s. Syon House continues to host corporate and private events including dinners, drinks receptions, meetings and promotions for both UK and International clients.

The Great Hall, State Dining Room and Duke's Private Dining Room are licensed for civil wedding ceremonies. The Inner Courtyard Garden with its pretty central fountain and parterres of white scented flowers, located at the centre of Syon House, plays host to post ceremony drinks. Alternatively, if the weather is unkind, drinks can be held in the Colonnade.

Evening wedding receptions and private parties are still held from Spring to Autumn in the Great Conservatory. Marquees in the parkland make an idyllic "rural" setting for larger corporate and private functions such as balls, gala dinners, exhibitions, team building events and conferences.

The expert wedding and events team are skilled in organising many different types of elegant celebrations, from award ceremonies and banquets, to weddings and private parties, all delivered in true Syon Park style.

*Pride and Prejudice and Zombies.*
*Courtesy of ... International UK Ltd.*

# SYON PARK
# IN FILMS

*Syon Park's unique historic buildings and landscaped parkland on the river Thames, so close to London and major studios, makes it a favourite location for feature films, television productions and photo shoots.*

Most recent feature films have included: Disney's Alice Through The Looking Glass, Pride and Prejudice With Zombies, Bollywood film Tab Jak Hai Jan and historic drama, Belle. There have been many television productions filmed at Syon and shown throughout the world, including Downton Abbey, Mr Selfridge, and Kiefer Sutherland's 24: Live Another Day. Syon's fabulously rich Robert Adam rooms have been the backdrop for many high fashion photo shoots with famous subjects and photographers such as Mario Testino.

*Alice Through the Looking Glass 2014.*
*© 2016 Disney Enterprises Inc. All Rights Reserved.*

Striking images have graced magazines like Vogue, Tatler and Harper's Bazaar. Behind the scenes promotional films can also be seen on You Tube.

From large scale productions such as Universal Pictures', The Wolfman, to award winning TV documentaries, Syon's filming legacy is impressive and there has been an ongoing family interest in film, most notably by Henry, 11th Duke of Northumberland.

*Harper's Bazaar UK / Norman Jean Roy*

*Henry, 11th Duke of Northumberland (1988-1995) had a passion for film-making and owned a production company, Hotspur Productions. His company was associated in the making of the feature film Lost in Africa and Harry Percy (as he appears on the credits) played the part of George.*

Modern classic films such as The Madness of King George and Robert Altman's Gosford Park were filmed in the Long Gallery, Red Drawing Room and the upstairs bedrooms, as were BBC period dramas such as The Lost Prince and Sense and Sensibility.

# RESTORATION AND RENEWAL

*There have been few periods over the last 600 years when building or restoration works have not been underway in some shape or form at Syon. In recent years, the need for restoration has become increasingly pressing, and a series of major and minor works have been undertaken. In most cases, original materials and techniques are used, and all works are informed and guided by rigorous historical research.*

The biggest single project has been the complete re-roofing of Syon House, with the 19th century lead being replaced and extensive masonry works carried out. Most dramatically, the great Percy lion on the east front, originally from Northumberland House, was removed for restoration and re-installed in the summer of 2012.

Inside the House, works are often more delicate, and here the emphasis is on the careful cleaning and reinstatement of original features, whether paintings, wall hangings, or decorative features. In association with these works, obsolete and occasionally unsafe lighting has been replaced with specialist fittings which show the House at its best, without damaging the artefacts on display.

During the early 2000s a comprehensive masterplan for Syon was developed, culminating in the construction and opening of the Syon Hotel, and the removal of inappropriate modern structures, followed by restoration of the landscape. The 1960s Conference Centre to the north of the Great Conservatory was removed in 2010-11, and the Serpentine River restored to the original Brown layout.

In 2012 the Grade II listed iron bridge by James Wyatt across the Outer Lake was extensively restored, and there are plans to carry out similar works to Robert Adam's Lion Gate. Major works have also been carried out to the masonry and glazing on the Great Conservatory and will continue in years to come.